Love Test

WHAT GOD'S HIGH-LEVEL LOVE LOOKS LIKE WHEN RELEASED THROUGH *YOU*

Rick Renner

Unless otherwise indicated, all Scripture quotations are taken from the *King James Version* of the Bible.

Scriptures marked *NKJV* are taken from the *New King James Version* of the Bible © 1979, 1980, 1982 by Thomas Nelson, Inc. All rights reserved.

Scripture quotations marked *NLT* are taken from the Holy Bible, *New Living Translation,* copyright 1996, 2004. Used by permission of Tyndale House Publishers, Inc., Wheaton, Illinois 60189. All rights reserved.

The Love Test:
What God's High-Level Love Looks Like
    When Released Through YOU
ISBN: 978-1-68031206-5
Copyright © 2017 by Rick Renner
8316 E. 73rd St.
Tulsa, OK 74133

Published by Harrison House Publishers
Shippensburg, PA 17257
www.harrisonhouse.com

5 6 7 / 23 22 21

Editorial Consultant: Cynthia D. Hansen
Text Design: Lisa Simpson,
    www.SimpsonProductions.net

Though I speak with the tongues
of men and of angels,
and have not charity,
I am become as sounding brass,
or a tinkling cymbal.
And though I have the gift of prophecy,
and understand all mysteries,
and all knowledge;
and though I have all faith,
so that I could remove mountains,
and have not charity,
I am nothing.
And though I bestow all my goods
to feed the poor,
and though I give my body to be burned,
and have not charity,
it profiteth me nothing.
Charity suffereth long,
and is kind; charity envieth not;
charity vaunteth not itself, is not puffed up,
doth not behave itself unseemly,
seeketh not her own,
is not easily provoked, thinketh no evil;
Rejoiceth not in iniquity,
but rejoiceth in the truth;
beareth all things, believeth all things,
hopeth all things, endureth all things.
Charity never faileth....

1 Corinthians 13:1-8

CONTENTS

5

1

ARE YOU A SOUNDING BRASS OR A TINKLING CYMBAL?

Though I speak with the tongues of men and of angels and have not charity, I am become as sounding brass, or a tinkling cymbal.

— 1 Corinthians 13:1

There is no force greater in all of creation than the love of God. The Bible says that God's perfect love has the power both to eradicate the presence of fear (*see* 1 John 4:18) and to fuel the operation of faith in our lives (*see* Galatians 5:6). And love is not just a character quality that God possesses and imparts to us in

7

the new birth. The Bible says that God actually *is* Love (*see* 1 John 4:8).

That means when you received Jesus as your Lord and Savior, Love Himself was shed abroad in your heart! Now He dwells within you to empower you to live a life of love, just as Jesus did when He walked this earth.

Because the seed of God's Word has been sown into your own human spirit, this divine love is within you all the time. If you will let the Spirit of God release it from your heart, you will begin to experience the response of love as it wells up from deep within. And as you allow God's love to flow out of your life to others, it will transform your character to become more like Jesus Christ.

With all of that in mind, we're going to delve into First Corinthians 13, which is the portion of Scripture that provides the best in-depth description of God's kind of love — translated "charity" in the *King James Version*. This word "charity" ("love") is the Greek word *agape*. It's actually a complex term to define. But I call it *high-level love* because there is no higher, finer, or more excellent love than *agape* love. It is the highest form of love — a sacrificial type of love that moves one to action.

So what does a life of high-level love look like? What does it mean to walk in the *agape* love of God? Nowhere in the Bible is that question answered more thoroughly than in this chapter in First Corinthians that we're about to explore. I believe that in the process of this discussion, you'll come to a clearer understanding of how to express the love of God in every situation you face in life. And as you apply what you learn to your daily life, you'll find yourself better equipped and more empowered to respond in every situation according to the law of love.

'Though I Speak...
and Have Not Charity'

So let's begin with the very first verse in First Corinthians 13, which shows us the priority God puts not only on the words we speak, but also on the heart motive behind our words. Love must be the force that empowers our words. If there is any taint of self-focus, self-promotion, or "self *anything*" in what we speak, Paul stressed in First Corinthians 13:1 that we are acting outside of the law of love and our words actually *grate* against the ears of God.

Just think about your own experience. Have you ever been around people who talked incessantly about their own accomplishments and talents? After a while, did you finally just tune them out because their words sounded like noise to you?

During the apostle Paul's ministry in the city of Corinth, he encountered a group of believers who were just like this. These people held their spirituality in extremely high regard and boasted about it at every possible opportunity. However, Paul was not impressed because despite their "super-spirituality," they did not walk in love. In fact, their deficit of love bothered him so deeply that he alluded to it in his first epistle to the Corinthian church, saying, "Though I speak with the tongues of men and of angels, and have not charity, I am become as sounding brass, or a tinkling cymbal" (1 Corinthians 13:1).

The phrase "sounding brass" is crucial to understanding Paul's intention in this verse. The word "brass" is the Greek word *chalkos*, an old word that referred to *bronze*, which is made by mixing with a small amount of tin into molten copper. Ancient metallurgists added tin to copper to create a material that was stronger and more durable than either of its components on their own.

However, this combination also had the added effect of causing the final product to make a particularly loud, hollow, clanging sound when beaten. That's why Paul also used the word "sounding" to describe it in this verse. It is a translation of the Greek word *echo*, which denotes *loud noise that reverberates or echoes*. Used together, the words "sounding brass" conjure the image of *a person beating a piece of bronze to produce a hollow, annoying, irritating echo that seems to eternally reverberate.*

So what exactly was Paul trying to convey with this imagery? The picture of "sounding brass" was actually an illustration the apostle borrowed from the pagan culture of Corinth. He used it in this verse to make a point about believers who brag about their spirituality but demonstrate no love.

The city of Corinth was deeply devoted to pagan religions. In fact, in terms of paganism and idolatry, Corinth stands out as one of the wickedest cities that may have ever existed. Night and day, the city's pagan temples were filled with worshipers who sought to connect with the spirit realm through all manner of strange and perverse rituals. They danced wildly under the influence of wine and drugs to the loud, rhythmic beat of bronze drums. As the pagan priests beat the metal at faster and faster tempos, the cacophonous sounds drove the worshipers over the edge into a frenzied state of spiritual ecstasy.

The citizens of Corinth were *very* familiar with this loud, obnoxious ritual, and although they believed it was an essential part of their worship, these piercing sounds were a constant irritation and nuisance to them as they went about their daily routines. They could never escape the constant, metallic clanging that permeated the city. Over time, this well-known and commonly loathed noise became the very thing people used to describe *a person who talked incessantly.*

This is exactly what Paul was talking about in First Corinthians 13:1. The "super-spiritual" believers he encountered in Corinth were as aggravating as the frenzied brass drumming that echoed ceaselessly from the city's temples. These people talked *a lot* about their spiritual walk, but their actions did not match their conversation. Therefore, Paul said their boasts were merely empty, shallow, banging *noises* that eventually irritated everyone who was near enough to hear them.

In verse 1, Paul also likened these "super-spiritual" believers to "a tinkling cymbal." This phrase is actually a very poor translation, as the language is much stronger in the original Greek. The word "tinkling" is the word *alalazon*, which means *to clash* or *to crash loudly*, and the word "cymbal" comes from the Greek word *kumbalon*, which is simply the Greek word for *cymbals.*

When these two words are compounded, the new word describes *a constant, loud clashing of cymbals* rather than a subdued "tinkling." With this imagery, Paul intended to call to mind the clashing cymbals that Jewish soldiers played just before they went to war. The loud clashing of those cymbals was a call to arms and a signal that it was time to fight!

According to Paul, people who claim great spirituality but don't demonstrate love are as irritating and nerve-racking as a "sounding brass" (*chalkos echo*), and they arouse the mind and emotions for fleshly war like a "tinkling cymbal" (*kumbalon alalazon*). As these people prattle on and on — heaping shallow, boastful, self-glorifying words upon themselves — it can almost make you want to stand up and fight. But don't do it!

When you deal with people like that, you need to pray for patience. If a door opens for you to speak the truth in love, tell them how they are coming across to others. However, if they are unwilling to listen and change, ask God to show you a way to graciously remove yourself from the difficult encounter.

Be the Example
of What God's Love Looks Like

From time to time, you will have to interact with arrogant people who lack self-awareness and don't respond in love, so you might as well learn how to deal with them. Instead of focusing all your prayers on how to change these people, ask God to change *you* so you can respond to them in a spirit of love. They may have never seen true spirituality and therefore may not know what it looks like or how it sounds. If so, this is your opportunity to show them *the real deal!*

Don't wait until a person's incessant boasting drives you to the point of lashing out in anger. Long before you ever get there, go to the Lord and ask Him to give you His heart for that person. When you have God's heart and mind about the situation, you'll be able to deal with it from the heart of Jesus — *the heart of love.*

But here's a question: What should you do if *you* fit Paul's description in First Corinthians 13:1? Think about it for a moment. Do your words act like a repellent that drives people away from you? If so, you need to pay close attention to what you've just read. If you've noticed that people are avoiding you, find out the reason why. Go to someone you trust and ask, "Would you please tell me what I am doing that is driving people away from me?" If you're going to ask this question, however, be prepared to gracefully receive the answer and correct your character, your words, and your life.

The last thing you want to be is a sounding brass or a tinkling cymbal! And the very *first* thing you want to do is demonstrate to others the selfless, sacrificial love of God. Therefore, it's always a good idea to go to the Lord and ask Him to reveal any problems in your words or actions that need to change. *And if the Holy Spirit does reveal something to you, make it your top priority to bring correction to your life!*

2

~ᢙ

LOVE IS PATIENT AND KIND

**Charity suffereth long, and is kind;
charity envieth not....**

— 1 Corinthians 13:4

O ver the course of the next chapters, I will
speak to you about Paul's words in First
Corinthians 13:4-8, where he taught us about
how to walk in love. These powerful verses
are like a mirror that reveals the condition of
your spiritual walk. If you will be brave enough
to look honestly into that mirror, you will
discover whether or not your life is a reflection
of the high-level kind of love God wants you
to exhibit toward others. If you learn that your

life is a reflection of this love, you can praise God for the great growth and maturity you've attained thus far. But if you find that your life does *not* reflect the kind of love God wants you to possess, take it as a signal from Heaven that you need to change and become more like Jesus!

In First Corinthians 13:4-8, Paul wrote, "Charity suffereth long, and is kind; charity envieth not; charity vaunteth not itself, is not puffed up, doth not behave itself unseemly, seeketh not her own, is not easily provoked, thinketh no evil; rejoiceth not in iniquity, but rejoiceth in the truth; beareth all things, believeth all things, hopeth all things, endureth all things. Charity never faileth...."

The word "charity" repeated in these verses is a translation of the Greek word *agape*, a powerful word used throughout the New Testament to describe *high-level, God-like love.* Here the apostle Paul tells us about primary marks or

20

characteristics of *agape* love. We are going to be looking at each one of these points. However, before we examine the specific manifestations of *agape* love, let's first look at the word *agape* itself, for it describes a very special kind of love, unlike any other in the world.

The word *agape* refers to the highest level of love in this world, and it is exactly the kind of love God expects every believer to demonstrate in his or her life. It describes a love so completely different from what the world offers that it is used in the New Testament only to describe God's love and the love that should flow from the hearts of believers.

Agape is a divine, unconditional love that gives and gives and gives, even if it's never thanked or acknowledged. In fact, you could say that *agape* is rooted in a decision to keep on loving, regardless of a recipient's response. It is the highest, noblest, and purest form of love that exists.

The Characteristics of *Agape* Love

Paul began his description of *agape* love in First Corinthians 13:4 by saying, "Charity *suffereth long*...." The words "suffereth long" are taken from the Greek word *makrothumia*, a compound of the words *makros* and *thumos*. The word *makros* indicates something that is *long, distant, far, remote*, or *of long duration*. The word *thumos* means *anger*, but it also embodies the idea of *swelling emotions* or *a strong and growing passion about something*.

When these two words are compounded into one, they form the word *makrothumia*, meaning *the patient restraint of anger, forbearance, patience*, or *long-suffering*. It depicts someone who is *prepared to wait patiently for a person to come around, make progress, or change*. This is the picture of a person whose feelings for someone else are so passionate that he doesn't easily give up or bow out when a situation

22

gets difficult. Instead, he keeps on going and going and going, even though the other person doesn't quickly respond to him.

So when Paul said, "Charity suffereth long," his words could be rendered:

"Love patiently and passionately bears with others for as long as patience is needed...."

Dear friend, *agape* love doesn't throw in the towel and quit. In fact, the harder the fight and the longer the struggle, the more committed *agape* love becomes. This, of course, is contrary to human nature, which says, "I'm sick and tired of waiting and believing. If that person doesn't come around pretty soon, I'm finished with this relationship."

Are you currently in a relationship that tests your patience? Are you tempted to throw up your arms in exasperation? If so, you need a good dose of *agape* love to be released in you! According to Romans 5:5, the *agape* love of God has already been "shed abroad" in your heart by the Holy Spirit. This means you don't have to come up with supernatural love on your own. You already have it in your heart.

The words "shed abroad" are from the Greek word *ekcheo*, which denotes *a pouring forth*, *a discharge*, *a spilling out*, or *something that is dispersed in abundance*. In other words, God has magnificently bestowed on you the love you need to be longsuffering in any relationship or situation. Ask the Holy Spirit to help you reveal God's love, and it will cause you to be patient toward that person who has frustrated you so much.

It's just a fact that human nature is short-tempered and intolerant, but *agape* is slow to anger, slow to wrath, and doesn't know how to quit! It supernaturally becomes stronger and more committed. This is a miraculous love — *a love that transforms and changes people's lives.*

Love Is Kind

Paul continued in verse 4 by listing the next characteristic of *agape* love: "Charity suffereth long, and *is kind*...." The word "kind" is the Greek word *chresteuomai*, which means to be *adaptable or compliant to the needs of others.* When *agape* is working in your life, you don't demand that others be like you. Instead, *agape* makes you want to bend over backwards to become what others need you to be for them! Thus, the word "kind" portrays *a willingness to serve and change in order to meet the needs of others.* This is completely opposite of selfishness and self-centeredness.

**So when Paul wrote that love is "kind,"
an expanded interpretation
of this phrase would mean:**

> *"…Love doesn't demand others to be like itself; rather, it is so focused on the needs of others that it bends over backwards to become what others need it to be.…"*

Given Paul's intention when he wrote that love is kind, we must look into the mirror and ask ourselves, *Do I become what others need me to be, or do I demand that others be like me?* Real *agape* love doesn't think of itself first. Instead, it is always reaching out, thinking and focusing primarily on the needs of others. The person walking in *agape* love adapts to those around him in order to touch them, help them, and impact them in a meaningful way.

Love Is Not Self-Absorbed

Next Paul said, "…Charity envieth not…." The word "envieth" is the Greek word *zelos*, which portrays *a person who is radically consumed with his own desires and plans.* This is a person who is so bent on getting his own way that he is willing to sacrifice anything or anyone to get it. You might describe this person as being *ambitious and self-centered*. He is so consumed with himself that he doesn't ever think of the needs or desires of others. His own plans are paramount in his mind, and everyone else comes after him.

**Therefore, when Paul said,
"...Charity envieth not...,"
his words could actually be rendered:**

"...Love is not ambitious, self-centered, or so consumed with itself that it never thinks of the needs or desires that others possess...."

I long so much to see this terrible flaw uprooted from all of our lives! You see, real *agape* love thinks other people rather than itself. So examine your relationships at home, at church, and at work, and ask yourself, "Am I committed to blessing others and helping them succeed, or do I mostly think about furthering my own agenda?"

When all these Greek words and phrases are taken together, an expanded interpretive translation of First Corinthians 13:4 could read:

"Love passionately bears with others for as long as patience is needed. Love doesn't demand others to be like itself. Rather, it is so focused on the needs of others that it bends over backwards to become what others need it to be. Love is not ambitious, self-centered, or so consumed with itself that it never thinks of other people's needs and desires...."

Now that you know what the Bible means when it says love is patient, kind, and not envious, look into God's "mirror" and see what it tells you about your own life today. Do you demonstrate these characteristics of divine love in your life? Are you passionately patient with others? Do you bend over backwards to be what other people need you to be? Are you more focused on people around you than on yourself? If your answer is "yes" to these questions, then praise God for the great growth and spiritual maturity you have gained in your life.

On the other hand, if you see that your life is *not* reflecting these attributes of God's love, you still have something to rejoice about — you can be thankful that God has revealed this deficiency to you. *Now you can ask Him to help change you and make you more like Jesus!*

3

～ᴄ℘

LOVE IS NOT PUFFED UP

> **...Charity vaunteth not itself, is not puffed up, Doth not behave itself unseemly....**
>
> — **1 Corinthians 13:4,5**

As we saw in Chapter 1, Paul alluded to Christians in the city of Corinth who boasted incessantly about their spiritual gifts and accomplishments but exhibited very little love in their lives (*see* Corinthians 13:1). Specifically, he said they were like a "sounding brass" and a "tinkling cymbal" — phrases that indicate these people talked *ad nauseum*, annoying others with their obnoxious, self-consumed chatter. Paul's description of these "super-spirituals" directly

31

ties into the next characteristic of high-level *agape* love he listed in verse 4: "Charity *vaunteth not itself….*"

The word "vaunteth" comes from the Greek word *perpereuomai*, which means *excessive self-talk* or *self-aggrandizing*. In other words, it describes *a person who endlessly promotes himself and exaggerates his own virtues.* His self-promotion is so outrageous that it borders on lying. If we wanted to use modern idioms, it would be accurate to say that this word *perpereuomai* pictures *a person who is full of hot air* or *a windbag*!

**The word "vaunteth"
is Paul's strong warning to let us know:**

> "*…Love doesn't go around talking about itself all the time, constantly exaggerating and embellishing the facts to make it look more important in the sight of others….*"

32

If you know anyone who acts like this, no doubt Paul's description immediately reminded you of that person. This character trait is so annoying that it's very difficult to ignore or forget a person who exudes it.

Even as I write, I am reminded of an individual who fits this description perfectly! When people see this man approaching them, they immediately begin looking for a way out. They know that once he gets hold of them, he will start talking endlessly about himself, his projects, his ideas, and his accomplishments. He boasts to such an extreme degree that it is simply obnoxious. The problem is, he doesn't seem to be aware how full of himself he actually is!

Once a mutual friend asked him, "Why don't you ever ask about anyone else? All you ever talk about is yourself and your own feats. Don't you think it would be good to show at least some interest in what others are doing?

Do you know how selfish you seem to be to other people?"

The man answered, "Is anyone else besides myself doing anything that is worth talking about? I'm the only one doing anything significant."

His reply was mind-boggling to me! This man was so self-absorbed that he couldn't even recognize the fact that there are other hard-working high-achievers in the Kingdom of God! His narcissism stems from toxic, deep-rooted insecurities, which have caused him to feel compelled to stretch the truth to a ridiculous extreme and brag about his own accomplishments in order to be accepted. He has sung his own praises for so long that none of his friends or family want to listen to his boasts for another minute! His total lack of concern for others and his complete preoccupation with himself have become offensive and disgusting to nearly everyone who knows him.

Some people exaggerate and boast end-lessly because they have a hidden agenda and want to gain a higher position of authority. In other cases, they hope to make an impression that will give them special status or recognition in the eyes of others. Or they may just feel driven to prove their worth, because they struggle with deep-rooted insecurities like the man I described. Regardless of the reason, this behavior is diametrically opposed to the manner in which *agape* love operates!

Agape love is so strong, so confident, and so sure of itself that it doesn't need to speak of itself or its accomplishments — even if those accomplishments are greater than anyone else's. Real *agape* love would never flaunt itself in this way; instead, it focuses on the accomplishments of others in order to build them up and make them feel more valuable and secure. Remember, *agape* isn't a self-focused love — it seeks to give and give in order to meet other people's needs.

Love Is Not Puffed Up

In verse 4, Paul listed another characteristic of *agape* love, saying, "Charity vaunteth not itself, is not *puffed up*...." This phrase "puffed up" is a translation of the Greek word *phusio*, which means *to be proud, to be swollen*, or *to be inflated*. Thus, this word vividly paints the picture of *a person who is filled with pride*. Paul warned that *agape* is never *phusio*, meaning it is never *deceived into thinking too highly of itself*, nor does it *arrogantly claim that it is better than others*. The word *phusio* also carries the notion of a *person who has an air of superiority and haughtiness* or *a person who is snooty* or *snobbish in his dealings with other people*.

Paul used the word *phusio* numerous times in his first epistle to the Corinthians, because pride was a recurring problem in that congregation. In First Corinthians 4:6 and 19, he used it to describe the *pride* and *arrogance* that was developing between wrangling members of the Corinthian church, each of whom believed that his or her particular leader was more important than other leaders.

At the time, this arrogance regarding leadership was the primary source of division, contention, and rivalry in the Corinthian church. In First Corinthians 5:2, Paul used *phusio* again after boldly confronting the Corinthian church for tolerating a grossly immoral situation among its members. Here Paul expressed his amazement that they could be "puffed up" in light of the ungodly relationship that was thriving right before their eyes. Finally, in First Corinthians 8:1 (*NKJV*), Paul used the word *phusio* when he said, "...Knowledge puffs up, but love edifies."

**When you consider the Greek meaning
of the phrase "puffed up," it becomes evident
that Paul was letting us know:**

*"...Love does not behave in a prideful,
arrogant, haughty, superior, snooty, snobbish, or clannish manner."*

Love Is Not Inconsiderate of Others

In verse 5, Paul told us the next characteristic of *agape* love, saying, "[Love] doth not
behave itself unseemly...." The Greek word
for "unseemly" is *aschemoneo*, an old word that
means *to act in an unbecoming manner*. It sug-
gests a *person who is tactless or thoughtless*. It also
expresses the notion of a *person who is careless
and inconsiderate of others*. Both his actions and
words tend to be rude and discourteous, and
he exhibits bad manners in the way he deals
with people.

38

Here is what the Holy Spirit is telling us:

"Love is not rude and discourteous. It is not careless or thoughtless, nor does it carry on in a fashion that would be considered insensitive to others...."

So how do you fare when you look into the mirror of God's Word today? Do you pass the love test, or have you come up short again? If you see that you have fallen short of the high-level love God wants you to possess and exhibit in your life, it's time for you to go back to the Lord and talk to Him about it again! Never stop going to Him, and the time will come when you know that you are walking continually in the high-level love He wants you to demonstrate in your life!

An expanded interpretive translation of the First Corinthians 13:4,5 could read:

"...Love doesn't go around talking about itself all the time, constantly exaggerating and embellishing the facts to make itself look more important in the sight of others. Love does not behave in a prideful, arrogant, haughty, superior, snooty, snobbish, or clannish manner. Love is not rude and discourteous. It is not careless or thoughtless, nor does it carry on in a fashion that would be considered insensitive to others...."

Is the Holy Spirit speaking to your heart about some things that need to change in your life? Is He showing you areas where you have:

- Exaggerated the truth to make yourself look better in the eyes of others?

- Acted in a prideful, haughty, snobbish, or clannish manner?

- Permitted yourself to act in a way that is not acceptable for someone who is striving toward godly excellence?

If your answer is *yes* to any of these questions, it's time for you to take immediate action! You need to spend some quality time with Jesus. Ask Him to forgive you, and let His blood cleanse you. Then ask the Holy Spirit to start the process of transforming you into the image of Jesus. *Don't stop until you think, see, and act like Jesus Christ — every moment of every day!*

4

~ఁ

LOVE IS NOT EASILY
PROVOKED

**[Charity] doth not behave itself
unseemly, seeketh not her own, is not
easily provoked, thinketh no evil....**

— 1 Corinthians 13:5

Paul continued his message about the high-level *agape* love of God by saying it "...*seeketh not her own*...." The word "seeketh" is the Greek word *zeteo*, which literally means *to seek*. However, it was commonly used in New Testament times to depict *a person who is so upset about not getting what he wants that he turns to the court system to sue or to demand that he gets his way.*

Instead of taking "no" for an answer, this person will search and investigate relentlessly in order to get what he wants, never giving up in his pursuit until his drive is satisfied. In fact, he's so bent on getting his way that he'll engage in all manner of immoral and questionable activities. He'll twist the facts, look for loopholes, put words in other people's mouths, try to hold others accountable for promises they never made, leap on administrative mistakes as opportunities to twist someone's arm, or seek various other methods to turn situations to his benefit. It is manipulation, plain and simple!

There is no doubt that Paul had the image of a manipulating, scheming person in his mind when he wrote this verse. Have you ever met such a person? Have you ever encountered a person who constantly schemed and manipulated to get what he or she wanted? The point

Paul was making in verse 5 is that love is not scheming or manipulating, for this kind of behavior is dishonest and untruthful. If you can't honestly state what you think or what you want, then don't say or do anything. Speaking half-truths and white lies or operating according to a secret agenda is not the way *agape* love behaves.

The Greek words in this text could be understood to mean:

"...Love does not manipulate situations or scheme and devise methods that will twist situations to its own advantage...."

Love Is Not Easily Provoked

Paul gave another characteristic of *agape* love in verse 5 when said that love "...is not easily provoked...." The word "provoked" in Greek is the word *paroxsuno*. It is a compound of *para*, meaning *alongside*, and *oxsus*, which means *to poke, to prick*, or *to stick with a sharpened instrument*. When compounded, the new word portrays *someone who comes alongside another and then begins to poke, prick, or stick that other person with some type of sharpened instrument*. He continues to poke and prod until the victim is provoked and a fight breaks out — *a conflict of the most serious order*.

We find the word *paroxsunos* used in a similar way in Acts 15:39, where Luke recorded a conflict that transpired between Paul and Barnabas. Barnabas wanted to take John Mark on the next journey, but Paul was against it because John Mark had already proven himself unfaithful on an earlier trip. As they debated the issue, the words they exchanged must have been very sharp because Luke wrote, "And the contention was so sharp (*paroxsuno*) between them...."

Luke's choice of words lets us know that Paul and Barnabas came alongside each other in close debate and then began to poke, prick, and jab each other with their words. The Greek language leaves no doubt that the conversation that ensued was extremely hot. In fact, this provocation was so severe that it disrupted their friendship and destroyed their partnership in ministry. Acts 15:39,40 relates, "...*Barnabas took Mark, and sailed unto Cyprus; and Paul chose Silas, and departed....*"

Interestingly, the word *oxsus* is also the Greek word for *vinegar*. In other words, Paul and Barnabas spoke to each other in words that were stringent, sharp, severe, sour, tart, bitter, and acrid. These words were so bitter that it left a sour taste in their mouths and their memories. I'm sure Paul remembered this experience vividly when he warned believers everywhere that love is "...not easily provoked...." He was speaking from *personal experience*. Having reaped the consequences of losing his temper and saying regrettable, acrid words in a moment of conflict, Paul warned us that *agape* love does not behave in this fashion.

An interpretive translation of Paul's words in First Corinthians 13:5 could read:

"…Love does not deliberately engage in actions or speak words that are so sharp, they cause an ugly or violent response.…"

Love Thinks No Evil

The next thing Paul said about *agape* love is that it "…thinketh no evil." The Greek word for "thinketh" is *logidzomai*, an accounting term that would be better translated *to count* or *to reckon*. It literally means to credit *to someone's account*. Before us is the image of a bookkeeper who meticulously keeps accurate financial records. But in this case, the bookkeeper is an offended person who keeps detailed records of every wrong that was ever done to him. Just

48

as a bookkeeper has an entry for every debit and credit on the books, this person painstakingly stores in his memory all the mistakes, faults, grievances, disappointments, failures, or perceived wrongdoings that people have made against him.

This is certainly not the way *agape* love behaves! To know how it does behave, simply look at the way God behaves toward *you*. Although He could drag up your past mistakes and hold them against you if He chose to do so, God doesn't do that! In fact, after He forgave you (*see* Psalm 103:3), He decided He wouldn't deal with you according to your sins or reward you according to your iniquities (*see* Psalm 103:10). God *doesn't* and *never will* choose to remember them.

Psalm 103:12 says, "As far as the east is from the west, so far hath he removed our transgressions from us." This means that God doesn't keep records of your past forgiven sins!

49

Once they are under the blood of Jesus, God separates them from you forever. That is how real *agape* love behaves.

So if you are ever tempted to keep mental records of the way someone has wronged you, be aware that you're not giving that person the same mercy God has afforded you. When you consider how much you have been forgiven, you will realize that you have no right to keep a record of someone else's mistakes!

**Paul's words "thinketh no evil"
should actually be translated:**

*"…Love does not deliberately keep records
of wrongs or past mistakes."*

Is there anyone you are holding hostage in your mind because he acted in a way that you deemed inappropriate? If that person wronged you, it's all right for you to confront him in love. But once you have dealt with the matter,

you need to release the offense and let it go —
just as Jesus has released you from your past and
now believes that you are on the right track!

If you have a hard time releasing people
from their past wrongs, it's a sign that you need
agape to be activated in your life. The fact that
you're flipping back through that old record of
past offenses again and again — bringing up
past grievances that should have been forgiven
and forgotten — means you're not perfected in
love! Throw away that ledger book! *Didn't God
throw away His ledger about your past?*

**With all these Greek words and phrases in mind,
an expanded interpretive translation
of verse 5 could read:**

> "...Love doesn't manipulate situations
> or scheme and devise methods that will
> twist situations to its own advantage;
> love does not deliberately engage in
> actions or speak words that are so sharp,

*they cause an ugly or violent response;
love doesn't deliberately keep records of
wrongs or past mistakes."*

How do you feel after looking into the
mirror of First Corinthians 13:5? Take the
time to carefully digest this message and let
Paul's words sink deep into your heart and soul.
God wants to change you, but before you can
change, you must first recognize what needs
to be fixed! If He is speaking to your heart,
don't rush from this quiet time with Him too
quickly. Stop everything you are doing, and
make it your most important matter of busi-
ness to get your heart right — first with the
Lord and then with others!

5

LOVE REJOICES WITH THE TRUTH

[Charity] rejoiceth not in iniquity, but rejoiceth in the truth.

— 1 Corinthians 13:6

Have you ever secretly rejoiced when you heard that someone you didn't like or disapproved of had gotten into some kind of trouble? Upon hearing of that person's hardship, perhaps you were tempted to think, *Serves him right! He deserves what he's getting! After what he did to me and to so many others, he deserves a little punishment!* If this describes you, friend, let me tell you that this is not the way God's love reacts to such situations!

Allow me to share an illustration from my own life. There was once a man who seriously wronged our ministry. What he did to us was so wrong that he could have been judged in a court of law and sentenced to prison for his actions. But my wife and I decided to let it go and pray for God to deal with this individual. We knew that if he didn't repent, he would come under severe judgment. In the years since that event occurred, this man has come into many miserable hardships in his life. His children fell into terrible sin; he lost everything financially; and almost all who knew him turned their back on him.

When I first met this man, he went to church and had a successful ministry. The touch of God was on his life. But over time, he became a mess of a man — one of the saddest stories I personally have ever known. When this individual first began to fall into trouble, I found myself privately wanting to rejoice that judgment had finally come his way. Then the Holy Spirit convicted my heart, and I realized that rejoicing in this man's trouble was not the way the love of God behaves. I began to inwardly mourn over the condition of this man who had once been so mightily used by God.

Love Does Not Rejoice in Iniquity

In First Corinthians 13:6, Paul wrote that love "...rejoiceth not in iniquity, but rejoiceth in the truth." The phrase "rejoiceth not" comes from the Greek phrase *ou chairei*. The word *ou* means *no* or *not*, and the word *chairei* is from the word *chairo*, which is the Greek word for *joy*. It is the picture of a person who is euphoric over something that has happened. Other words to describe *chairo* would be *overjoyed, elated, ecstatic, exhilarated, thrilled, jubilant,* or even *rapturous*. The word "iniquity" is the

Greek word *adikos*, which conveys the idea of *an injustice* or *something that is wrong or bad*.

**The entire phrase *ou chairei*
could be translated in the following way:**

*"Love does not feel overjoyed when it sees
an injustice done to someone else...."*

My secret desire to rejoice at this other man's hardships was completely contrary to the loving nature of God. Even though he had done wrong to me and to many others in the Christian community, the right response was to pray for his restoration. *Agape* love simply doesn't rejoice at someone else's misfortunes.

Love Rejoices With the Truth

Then Paul went on to tell us that when someone else gains some kind of advantage in life that we have been desiring, *agape* love rejoices with his victory! The word "rejoice" is

56

again the Greek word *chairo*, the same word used above.

This means the second part of this verse could be translated:

"...Love is elated, thrilled, ecstatic, and overjoyed with the truth."

How you respond to other people's troubles and blessings reveals a great deal about your true level of spiritual maturity. So ask yourself:

- *Do I rejoice when I hear bad news about someone who did me wrong in the past? Or does it break my heart to hear about the problems that person is facing?*

- *When someone steps into the blessing I've been believing for in my own life, am I elated for that person, or does it make me turn green with envy?*

- *When I see other people blessed with what I have longed to receive myself — am I able to truly rejoice with them? Does it thrill me to know that other people are moving upward in life? Or does it threaten me and make me sad?*

I encourage you to ask the Holy Spirit to deal with your heart about these issues. Take a little time today to let God's Spirit search your heart and show you the areas in your life where you need to grow in love.

6

⁓

LOVE BEARS, BELIEVES, HOPES, AND ENDURES ALL THINGS

[Charity] beareth all things, believeth all things hopeth all things, endureth all things.

— 1 Corinthians 13:7

In First Corinthians 13:7, Paul provided the next four characteristics that tell us what *agape* love looks like when lived out through a believer's life. Paul explained that genuine, God-like love *"beareth all things, believeth all things, hopeth all things, endureth all things."*

Love Bears All Things

Let's begin with the phrase *"beareth all things."* The word "beareth" is the Greek word *stego*, which means *to cover*, exactly as a roof covers a house. Inherent in this word *stego* is the concept of *protection*, exactly as a roof protects the inhabitants of a house from exposure to the outside influences of weather. The roof of a house is designed to shield people from storms, hurricanes, tornadoes, rain, hail, snow, wind, blistering hot temperatures, and so on. This protection is vital for survival in most climates, preventing people from either freezing to death or collapsing from prolonged exposure to sunlight and heat.

By using this word *stego* ("beareth"), the apostle Paul gave us a powerful illustration. First, we must understand that there are many different seasons to life, and not all seasons are pleasurable. In fact, some seasons of life are very stormy and difficult. There are moments when external circumstances assail us from without, and if we have no shield to guard us during these stormy times, it becomes much more difficult for us to survive spiritually.

Paul's use of the word *stego* in verse 7 stresses the truth that *agape* love protects us from the difficult times in our lives. Like the roof of a house, a friend who moves in the *agape* love of God will stay near you when you experience troubled times, hovering over you to protect you from the storms of life. Rather than expose you and your flaws to the view of others, they will *conceal, cover*, and *protect* you, for real *agape* love is always there in times of trouble to lend support.

The phrase "beareth all things" could be translated:

"Love protects, shields, guards, covers, conceals, and safeguards people from exposure...."

Love Believes All Things

Paul continued by saying *agape* love "*...believeth all things*...." The word "believeth" is actually the word *pisteuei*, which is the Greek word meaning *to put one's faith or trust in something or someone*. The tense used in the Greek text lets us know that this is a constant, continuous entrusting of one's faith in something or someone. It is a "never-give-up" kind of belief that something will turn out the very best. Therefore, this phrase in verse seven could actually be taken to mean that love *believes the best in every situation*.

Don't misunderstand; *agape* love isn't stupid, nor is it blind. It sees everything — the good, the bad, and the ugly. But because *agape* is filled with faith, it pushes the disconcerting, disturbing, negative realities out of the way. This doesn't mean *agape* ignores problems or challenges. It just makes a choice to see beyond the problems and conflicts and strain forward to see the highest potential that resides in every person.

Let's consider this principle in the context of your children. Perhaps it is true that they are having problems right now or that they have done some things in the past they shouldn't have done. But there is still hope! You simply cannot give up believing that they will turn around! Although the past may have been filled with troubled times, the future is bright for those who believe God!

Therefore, *agape* continually presses ahead full of faith — reaching forward by faith to see the other person whole, sound, healed, saved, redeemed, and right in the middle of God's will for his or her life. You see, the *agape* love of God just doesn't know how to quit! It hangs on even when the going gets tough. It just keeps believing the very best, no matter what.

So I urge you to take a good, honest look at yourself to see if you are operating in this kind of *agape* love. Do you strain forward to believe the best, or do you have a habit of picking people apart and pointing out all their flaws and weaknesses? Never forget that love believes the best!

The phrase "believeth all things" could be translated:

"...Love strains forward with all its might to believe the very best in every situation...."

Love Expects the Best in People

Next Paul wrote that love "...*hopeth all things*...." The Greek word for "hopeth" is the word *elpidzo*, which depicts not only *a hope*, but *an expectation of good things*. This means that rather than assuming failure or a bad result in someone's life, the *agape* love of God always expects the best. In fact, it not only expects the best — it is filled with an anticipation to see the manifestation of the thing hoped for.

The phrase "hopeth all things" could be taken to mean:

"...Love always expects and anticipates the best in others and the best for others...."

Love Endures

Paul also said love *"...endureth all things."* The word "endureth" is the Greek word *hupomeno*, which is a compound of the words *hupo* and *meno*. The word *hupo* means *under*, and the word *meno*, means *to stay* or *to abide*. When compounded, the new word *hupomeno* depicts the attitude of *a person who is under a heavy load but refuses to surrender to defeat because he knows he is in his proper place.* Because this person knows he is where he's supposed to be, he has therefore resolved *to stay put* and *refuse to move*, no matter what comes against him!

This means *agape* never quits or throws in the towel. Real *agape* says, "I'm committed to be here — to stay with you and to work it out, regardless of the cost or the time involved. I'm not quitting. I am here to stay!" This kind of love is completely contrary to the flesh, which says, "I've done all I'm going to do. I'm not wasting any more of my life. I'm finished, and I'm leaving!"

A contemporary translation of the phrase "endureth all things" could be the following:

"…Love never quits, never surrenders, and never gives up."

As you look into the mirror of God's Word and examine the characteristics of *agape* love, can you say that this kind of love is operating in your life? Could others say that you have been a "roof" for them — protecting, covering, concealing, and guarding them during the hard and difficult seasons of their lives? Would

others say you believe the best about people,
or that you tend to be nit-picky and critical of
others? Have you made the decision to "stick it
out," regardless of how long it takes?

An expanded interpretive translation could read:

*"Love protects, shields, guards, covers, con-
ceals, and safeguards people from exposure.
Love strains forward with all its might
to believe the very best in every situation.
Love always expects and anticipates the
best in others and the best for others. Love
never quits, never surrenders, and never
gives up."*

I want to encourage you to make the
decision: From this moment forward, you are
committed to operating in this high-level *agape*
love of God. His love is already shed abroad in
your heart by the Holy Spirit, so now it's up to
you. Every day, no matter what challenge you

encounter, you can choose to open your heart and allow this divine river of love to flow forth from you to others. The power of that river will shift atmospheres, impact people's hearts, and make a way for God's will to be done in every situation.

7

LOVE NEVER FAILS

Charity never faileth....

— 1 Corinthians 13:8

Paul concluded his powerful message on *agape* love in First Corinthians 13:8 by affirming that love "never *faileth*." The word "faileth" is the Greek word *pipto*, meaning *to fall from a high position*. It was also used on rare occasions to depict *a warrior who fell in battle*. In many contexts, the word *pipto* is used to depict *falling into ruin, destruction, misfortune, or disappointment*. Paul used this word to affirm the eternal truth that love never *disappoints* or *fails*.

It is simply the truth that human beings often fail each other. I'm sure you have felt let down by someone else at some point along the way. You'll also have to admit that you've been guilty of letting others down as well. But *agape* love — God's love — never disappoints, never fails, and never lets anyone down. It is a love that can *always* be depended on and is *always* reliable.

People you know and respect may occasionally fall from the high position they hold in life — and that can be an emotionally difficult experience when you see it happen. Other times, fellow warriors may get wounded in battle or stumble into some kind of misfortune that disappoints you, and that can be painful as well. But you can be sure that the *agape* love of God will *never* fail you or let you down. This love is constant, unchanging, and unbendable. It is a love you will always find to be reliable and true — a love on which you can depend.

What Does *Agape* Love Look Like
in *Your* Life?

God wants you to learn to function in His high-level love, which is why the Holy Spirit so carefully inspired the apostle Paul to write these famous words in First Corinthians 13:4-8. This passage of Scripture is God's mirror, designed for us to look into so we can see how well we fare at walking in the *agape* love of God.

I have compiled all the words, phrases, and translations we have been studying and placed them here as one complete text for you to read. Take a few minutes to read this text slowly; then ask yourself, *Do I pass the* agape *love test?*

The following is
an expanded interpretive translation
of First Corinthians 13:4-8:

"Love patiently and passionately bears with others for as long as needed.

Love doesn't demand others to be like itself; rather, it is so focused on the needs of others that it bends over backwards to become what others need it to be.

Love is not ambitious, self-centered, or so consumed with itself that it never thinks of the needs or desires that others possess.

Love doesn't go around talking about itself all the time, constantly exaggerating and embellishing the facts to make it look more important in the sight of others.

Love does not behave in a prideful, arrogant, haughty, superior, snooty, snobbish, or clannish manner.

Love is not rude and discourteous — it is not careless or thoughtless, nor does it carry on in a fashion that would be considered insensitive to others.

Love does not manipulate situations or scheme and devise methods that will twist situations to its own advantage.

Love does not deliberately engage in actions or speak words that are so sharp that they cause an ugly or violent response.

Love does not deliberately keep records of wrongs or past mistakes.

Love does not feel overjoyed when it sees an injustice done to someone else.

Love is elated, thrilled, ecstatic, and over-joyed with the truth.

Love protects, shields, guards, covers, conceals, and safeguards people from exposure.

Love strains forward with all its might to believe the very best in every situation.

Love always expects and anticipates the best in others and the best for others.

Love never quits, never surrenders, and never gives up.

Love never disappoints, never fails, and never lets anyone down."

Do you manifest this type of love to others who are around you? If not, do you want to learn how to give people this type of love — God's love? Are you ready to grow, develop, and change in regard to walking in love?

I strongly encourage you to spend time in prayer about this issue of God's love in your life. Have an honest talk with the Lord about how well you relate to others and impact people with His love in every situation — even in difficult ones.

One day you will see Jesus face to face. And of all the questions He might ask you on that day, among the very most important will be this one: *"What did you do with My love that I placed in you?"* So determine today that you're

74

going to yield to the Holy Spirit's work in you from this day forward in this area of love. Then on that day, you will be able to look Jesus in the eyes and answer with confidence: *"Every day I got better at showing the world what Your love looks like!"*

SCRIPTURES ON LOVE
FOR PRAYER

Love

You have heard that it was said, "You shall love your neighbor and hate your enemy.' But I say to you, love your enemies, bless those who curse you, do good to those who hate you, and pray for those who spitefully use you and persecute you, that you may be sons of your Father in heaven; for He makes His sun rise on the evil and on the good, and sends rain on the just and on the unjust" (Matthew 5:43-45 *NKJV*).

This is my commandment, That ye love one another, as I have loved you (John 15:12).

I in them, and You in Me; that they may be made perfect in one, and that the world may know that You have sent Me, and have loved them as You have loved Me (John 17:23 *NKJV*).

I, therefore, the prisoner of the Lord, beseech you to walk worthy of the calling with which you were called, with all lowliness and gentleness, with longsuffering, bearing with one another in love, endeavoring to keep the unity of the Spirit in the bond of peace (Ephesians 4:1-3 *NKJV*).

Therefore be imitators of God as dear children. And walk in love, as Christ also has loved us and given Himself for us, an offering and a sacrifice to God for a sweet-smelling aroma (Ephesians 5:1,2 *NKJV*).

I pray that your love will overflow more and more, and that you will keep on growing in knowledge and understanding (Philippians 1:9 *NLT*).

If there be therefore any consolation in Christ, if any comfort of love, if any fellowship of the Spirit, if any bowels and mercies, fulfil ye my joy, that ye be likeminded, having the same love, being of one accord, of one mind. Let nothing be done through strife or vainglory; but in lowliness of mind let each esteem other better than themselves (Philippians 2:1-3).

Let us think of ways to motivate one another to acts of love and good works (Hebrews 10:24 *NLT*).

Forgiveness

Judge not, and ye shall not be judged: condemn not, and ye shall not be condemned: forgive, and ye shall be forgiven (Luke 6:37).

Forbearing one another, and forgiving one another, if any man have a quarrel against any: even as Christ forgave you, so also do ye (Colossians 3:13).

If we confess our sins, he is faithful and just to forgive us our sins, and to cleanse us from all unrighteousness (1 John 1:9).

Finally, all of you should be of one mind. Sympathize with each other. Love each other as brothers and sisters. Be tenderhearted, and keep a humble attitude. Don't repay evil for evil. Don't retaliate with insults when people insult you. Instead, pay them back with a blessing. That is what God has called you to do, and he will grant you his blessing (1 Peter 3:8-10 *NLT*).

PRAYER OF SALVATION

When Jesus Christ comes into your life, you are immediately emancipated — totally set free from the bondage of sin! If you have never received Jesus as your personal Savior, it is time to experience this new life for yourself. The first step to freedom is simple. Just pray this prayer from your heart:

Lord, I can never adequately thank You for all You did for me on the Cross. I am so undeserving, Jesus, but You came and gave Your life for me anyway.

I repent and turn from my sins right now. I receive You as my Savior, and I ask You to wash away my sin by Your precious blood. I thank You from the depths of my heart for doing what no one else could do for me. Had it not been for

Your willingness to lay down Your life for me, I would be eternally lost.

Thank You, Jesus, that I am now redeemed by Your blood. You bore my sin, my sickness, my pain, my lack of peace, and my suffering on the Cross. Your blood has covered my sin, washed me whiter than snow, and given me rightstanding with the Father. I have no need to be ashamed of my past sins, because I am now a new creature in You. Old things have passed away, and all things have become new because I am in Jesus Christ (1 Corinthians 5:17).

Because of You, Jesus, today I am forgiven; I am filled with peace; and I am a joint heir with You! Satan no longer has a right to lay any claim on me. From a grateful heart, I will faithfully serve You the rest of my days!

If you prayed this prayer from your heart, something amazing has happened to you. No longer a servant to sin, you are now a servant of Almighty God. The evil spirits that once exacted every ounce of your being and required your all-inclusive servitude no longer possess the authorization to control you or to dictate your destiny!

As a result of your decision to turn your life over to Jesus Christ, your eternal home has been decided forever. Heaven is now your permanent address.

God's Spirit has moved into your own human spirit, and you have become the "temple of God" (1 Corinthians 6:19). What a miracle! To think that God, by His Spirit, now lives inside of you!

Now you have a new Lord and Master, and His name is Jesus. From this moment on, the Spirit of God will work in you and supernaturally energize you to fulfill God's will for your life. Everything will change for you now — and it's all going to change for the best!

ABOUT THE AUTHOR

Rick Renner is a highly respected Bible teacher and leader in the international Christian community. Rick is the author of a long list of books, including the bestsellers *Dressed To Kill* and *Sparkling Gems From the Greek 1* and *2*, which have sold millions of copies worldwide. Rick's understanding of the Greek language and biblical history opens up the Scriptures in a unique way that enables readers to gain wisdom and insight while learning something brand new from the Word of God.

Today Rick is the senior pastor of the Moscow Good News Church and the founder of Media Mir, the first Christian television network in the former USSR that broadcasts the Gospel to countless Russian-speaking viewers around the world via multiple satellites and the Internet. He is also the founder and president of RENNER MINISTRIES, based in Tulsa, Oklahoma, and host to his TV program that is seen around the world in multiple languages. Rick leads this amazing work with his wife and lifelong ministry partner, Denise, along with the help of their sons and committed leadership team.

CONTACT RENNER MINISTRIES

For further information
about RENNER MINISTRIES, please contact
the RENNER MINISTRIES office nearest you,
or visit the ministry website at
www.renner.org

**ALL USA
CORRESPONDENCE:**
RENNER MINISTRIES
P. O. Box 702040
Tulsa, OK 74170-2040
(918) 496-3213
Or 1-800-RICK-593
Email: renner@renner.org
Website: www.renner.org

MOSCOW OFFICE:
RENNER MINISTRIES
P. O. Box 789
101000, Russia, Moscow
+7 (495) 727-14-67
Email: partner@rickrenner.ru
Website: www.rickrenner.ru

RIGA OFFICE:
RENNER MINISTRIES
Unijas 99
Riga LV-1084, Latvia
(371) 780-2150
Email: info@goodnews.lv

KIEV OFFICE:
RENNER MINISTRIES
P. O. Box 300
01001, Ukraine, Kiev
+38 (044) 451-8115
Email: partner@rickrenner.ru
Website: www.rickrenner.ru

OXFORD OFFICE:
RENNER MINISTRIES
Box 7, 266 Banbury Road
Oxford OX2 7DL, England
+44 (0) 1865 355509
Email: europe@renner.org

The Harrison House Vision

Proclaiming the truth and the power

of the Gospel of Jesus Christ with excellence.

Challenging Christians

to live victoriously,

grow spiritually,

know God intimately.

Connect with us on

Facebook @ HarrisonHousePublishers

and Instagram @ HarrisonHousePublishing

so you can stay up to date with news

about our books and our authors.

Visit us at **www.harrisonhouse.com**

for a complete product listing as well as

monthly specials for wholesale distribution.